Some Birds and Mammals of the Riverbank

by Kenneth Lilly

THE MEDICI SOCIETY LTD
LONDON 1983

Grey Heron *(Ardea cinerea)* HERON FAMILY

Size: The male and female are alike and stand about 30 in (76 cm) high with head raised.

Breeding: The female builds the nest. The male supplies her with the materials: sticks for the bulk of the nest and smaller twigs, dry grass, roots and reeds for the lining.

Herons breed in colonies or 'heronries' sometimes numbering more than 100 pairs. The heronry is usually sited in trees with several nests to a tree. Occasionally heronries may be sited on cliffs or reedbeds if no other suitable site is available.

The nest is built in February and three to five greenish blue eggs are laid in March. Both parents share the incubation period of some 25 days and the feeding and care of the baby herons, which fly when about eight weeks old. Two families are sometimes reared.

Habits: The heron is found wherever there is unpolluted water from the streams in the high hills down to the sea shore. Its food may consist of fish, frogs and any small water bird or mammal it can seize in its spear-like bill. Some vegetable matter and shell fish may also be eaten.

The heron is a stealthy, patient hunter, often wading up to its tummy in deep water, occasionally even swimming.

One heron would boldly fish in full view of a nearby kitchen window. One morning, it was 'spied' from the other side of this kitchen window by George, a huge shaggy Old English sheepdog who was the self-appointed guardian of his master's lake and the fish therein.

George announced the heron's presence with such loud and frantic barking, that he was let out to deal with the situation. Taking his duties seriously, he charged at full speed towards this brazen bird. Now, this thoughtful heron had the presence of mind to stand perfectly still, and due, perhaps, to the shaggy hair hanging over George's eyes, his head-long charge missed the stationary bird and almost took him head-first into the lake. Since this embarrassing experience, George has perfected a studied indifference to the heron's activities!

Reed Warbler *(Acrocephalus scirpaceus)* WARBLER FAMILY

Size: Length about 5 in (13 cm). The male and female are alike.

Breeding: The reed warbler is a summer visitor to Britain and the male bird arrives first. He will establish a territory in which the female, who arrives some two weeks later, will actually build the nest.

The nest is woven around the reed stems or other vegetation if necessary, some 18–50 in (45–127 cm) above the water level. It is made of grasses, reed flowers and seed heads, lined with any soft material available, such as wool, hairs and feathers.

While the female is busily engaged in constructing the nest, the male, seldom far from her side, appears to be offering her constant encouragement but – no help. If suitable nesting material is not readily available, she is not above stealing some from another bird's nest. Eventually the deep cup-shaped nest is finished and three to five greenish white eggs, spotted with grey, are laid.

The female, who does most of the incubating, sits low down in the nest to ensure that she and her eggs are not thrown out by the dangerously swaying, wind-swept, reed stems. The baby warblers may leave the nest after the tenth day but spend their time hiding among the dense reed stems and undergrowth for at least another week before eventually learning to fly. A second family may sometimes be reared.

Habits: The reed warbler is a very active little bird, though not very keen on flying. After the long flight from its winter home in tropical Africa, the reed warbler, once in Britain, seldom does more than fly low from one patch of reeds to another. It spends almost all its time moving about among the dense reed stems with quick, jerky movements in its constant search for food, which consists mainly of the insects found in abundance among the water plants. Fruit is also eaten when available.

Unfortunately for this little bird, its nest is often chosen by a cuckoo as the place in which to lay its own egg. Many reed warblers eggs and babies have been pushed out of the nest to make room for a baby cuckoo to grow to its enormous size. The little parent warblers, however, quite cheerfully work hard and do their very best to feed and care for their huge unknowingly adopted cuckoo baby.

The reed warbler has an apparently well-deserved reputation as a mimic. Keen bird watchers have at times become quite excited on hearing the song of several different birds in the same locality.

However, they have been disappointed and astonished to discover that the only bird about is a little reed warbler singing away to its own delight and everyone else's confusion.

Water Shrew *(Neomys fodiens)* SHREW FAMILY

Size: Head and body $3\text{–}3\frac{3}{4}$ in (about 8–9 cm). Tail about 3 in (8 cm) long. Weight about $\frac{1}{2}$ oz.

Breeding: Water shrews breed from April to September, but May or June seems to be the favoured period. Five to eight blind, hairless and helpless little babies are born in the nursery chamber, in a burrow dug into the riverbank. This nursery is lined with soft mosses, fine roots, grass and leaves to form a little snug round nest.

Baby water shrews grow up quickly and by the time they are six weeks old, they are quite capable of looking after themselves. Occasionally a second family is reared.

Habits: The water shrew is widely spread over much of England, Wales and Scotland, though not found at all in Ireland and some of the outer islands.

This little creature can be observed quite closely, provided one is quiet, because its eyesight is very poor and it relies chiefly on its hearing to be made aware of what is going on.

Its thick, dark fur, has a way of rètaining air so that when swimming, little tiny air bubbles give the fur a light silvery shimmering appearance which is most attractive. The toes are fringed with stiff hairs which help transform its feet into perfect paddles when in the water. The hind feet are much larger than the front ones and supply the real power for swimming, rather in the manner of an out-board motor. The tail is also adapted to assist in its swimming activities by two rows of silvery hairs on the underside which act as a keel and rudder.

The water shrew, like other shrews, must feed every two or three hours throughout the day and night, as it needs to consume its own bodyweight in food each day. This food will consist of water-dwelling insects, beetle larvae, snails, worms, frogs, fish and sometimes carrion. The shrew's bite has been found to be poisonous to

other small mammals. This may be the reason why some animals will kill a shrew but not eat it.

Shrews are very aggressive creatures and the males in particular will fight fiercely among themselves. Their courage is quite astonishing. I have seen a diminutive little shrew leap up to snap at a fully grown cat and sink its red-tipped teeth into the cat's paw. Whilst the bewildered cat was licking its wounded paw, the shrew scampered off and made good its escape.

Grey Wagtail *(Motacilla cinerea)*

WAGTAIL FAMILY

Size: Length about 7 in (18 cm). The male in spring has a striking black throat and a white stripe above and below the eye.

Breeding: During April or May, four to six eggs are laid and incubated mainly by the female. The eggs are buff and speckled grey and brown. The nest is usually built in a crevice in the riverbank or tree roots, in a bridge or indeed, any suitable structure provided it is close to water, preferably shallow, fast flowing water. Two families may be reared and very occasionally three.

The nest is constructed by the female with moss, leaves, fine roots and twigs to fill the available crevice and then lined with hair, fur and sometimes feathers. Both parents share the task of feeding the family.

Habits: The grey wagtail may be found in a variety of places, sometimes far from water such as gardens and farmyards, but there is no doubt that its favourite place is by the water. Here it can enjoy the wide variety of insects which, along with the occasional tiny fish, mollusc and beetle, are its favourite food.

The grey wagtail is a restless bird. Even when standing, the tail, as its name suggests, is wagging or, rather, bobbing up and down. Its movements are quick as it lightly moves from one twig, branch or stone to another. It will also run for short distances with short rapid strides with head moving backwards and forwards in time with its feet. Suddenly, in mid-stride, it will leap up to catch a flying insect. Sometimes it will do this from a perch in the manner of a flycatcher.

The male will defend its own territory quite fiercely, attacking any other males that may dare to venture on to his patch. This strong instinct to defend its territory probably accounts for the behaviour of one particular male that would spend most of its waking hours attacking its own reflection in a car wing-mirror. This activity went on for several days until finally, to prevent this brave little bird doing itself a serious injury, I covered the wing mirror with a cloth. Proudly believing that he had finally seen off this persistent intruder, he now felt free to resume his parental duties.

Ken Lilly

Otter *(Lutra lutra)* WEASEL FAMILY

Size: Overall length about 4 feet (120 cm), sometimes longer. Weight about 25 lb (12 kg). The male, or dog, is usually larger than the female, or bitch.

Breeding: The otter lives in a hole in the riverbank known as a 'holt'. The entrance is normally below the level of the water and overhung with tree roots or bank vegetation. A back door above the water level provides the otter with an alternative exit.

A small chamber off the main holt is used as a nursery where two or three blind babies are born. Their eyes open when they are about five weeks old and they venture out into the river-bank world when about eight weeks old. The babies, or cubs, swim naturally and seldom need much coaxing from their mother.

The cubs can be born at any time, but spring and summer seem to be the most popular times.

Habits: When the parents are no longer caring for the cubs, they separate and lead rather solitary lives. An otter will leave the holt at sunset and travel long distances, sometimes overland, in its search for profitable hunting grounds.

Of all land mammals, the otter is probably the most perfectly developed for a life spent mainly in the water. All four feet are webbed, and the long body is elegantly tapered and streamlined. When underwater, the ears close and become water-tight as it pursues the fish of which it is the equal in speed and agility. Fish and eels are probably its favourite food but it is also fond of shellfish, frogs, birds and small mammals.

When food is plentiful, an otter may store unfinished meals in a kind of 'larder'. I remember the time when a very unpleasant smell hung over the farm. After much wrinkling of noses and the frequent 'whew' it was decided that something must be done. The offending odour was finally traced to an old tree stump. There, the remains of fish, fowl and some indistinguishable fleshy matter was found and removed.

However, the smell returned and as the culprit was without doubt an otter, the hounds were called in. The otter must have seen them coming for when they got there, he wasn't. Eventually, in desperation, the stump was pulled out and all was once again sweetness and pure farmyard.

Ken Lilly

Teal *(Anas crecca)* DUCK FAMILY

Size: Length of both male and female about 14 in (35 cm).

Breeding: Eight to eleven eggs are usually laid sometime between April and July. The female, or duck, incubates the eggs and cares for the needs of the little ducklings. The male, or drake, may sometimes help look after the ducklings.

The nest is built by the duck and made with dry grasses and bracken, lined with dead leaves and small downy duck feathers. It is sited on the ground among rushes in marshland, wooded riverbanks, meadows or moorland, often well away from water and always well hidden.

One teal family I knew well would walk across two fields to the river. One field was inhabited by a mare and her foal. The foal's name was Happy and he would delight in escorting the teal family on their journey. The teal, however, were never quite certain of his intentions and their pace would quicken to a hurried but always dignified walking run as the riverbank drew nearer. Their eventual splash into the water was with obvious relief. Happy, left standing on the riverbank, always looked slightly bewildered and saddened by their apparent mistrust and lack of friendliness.

Habits: The teal is one of the smallest of the duck family and one of the most beautiful. After the breeding season, the drake loses his attractive colouring and markings and looks more like the duck for about three months. This phase is known as the 'eclipse'.

This little duck prefers shallow water, often near the riverbank. Here, it need only 'duck' its head under the water and present its tail to the sky in order to reach the various waterplants and small shrimp-like creatures which form its main diet. Insects and seeds are also eaten.

Although teal feed mainly at night, their presence during the day can be detected by a soft

contented quacking as they search for food under overhanging riverbank vegetation. When disturbed, teal take-off almost vertically and fly very fast and low, frequently swerving from one side to another.

Apart from the breeding season, teal can be found in pairs or small groups and sometimes large flocks of more than a hundred.

Moorhen *(Gallinula chloropus)* RAIL FAMILY

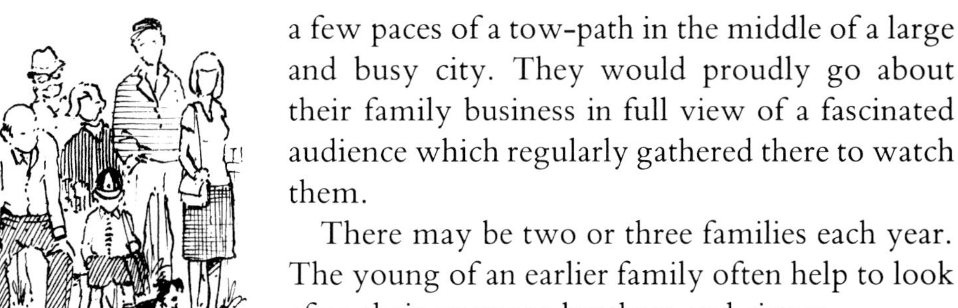

Size: Length about 13 in (33 cm). Male and female are alike.

Breeding: Moorhens normally pair for life and share the task of hatching the eggs and caring for the chicks. In March or April, five to eleven whitish buff eggs, speckled and blotched with dark brown are laid. Sometimes two females will lay their eggs in the same nest. This probably would account for some nests containing twenty or more eggs.

The nest is large and roughly constructed, usually of dead reeds and sedges. This is lined with dry grasses and sometimes decorated with flowers and other bits and pieces a moorhen may find attractive. It is normally built close to the water among vegetation. Occasionally the moorhen will nest in a nearby bush or tree, often taking over the old nest of another bird.

The nest is not always very well concealed. I remember well a pair of moorhens boldly building their nest and bringng up their family within a few paces of a tow-path in the middle of a large and busy city. They would proudly go about their family business in full view of a fascinated audience which regularly gathered there to watch them.

There may be two or three families each year. The young of an earlier family often help to look after their younger brothers and sisters.

Habits: The moorhen is likely to be found wherever there is fresh water. Its taste in food varies widely from water plants and small fish, to insects, worms, berries and fruit. Strangely enough, for a bird that spends most of its time in the water, it does not have webbed feet. Its toes are remarkably long and when walking, it cautiously lifts its feet high to prevent the long toes dragging on the ground. In water its movements are quick with head bobbing backwards and forwards and tail constantly flicking.

Although the moorhen will dive, it doesn't seem very happy about it and only remains underwater for a few seconds. It appears to be even less happy about flying and will do so only for a very short distance. When in a hurry, it prefers to half fly, half run, across the water.

Water Vole *(Arvicola amphibius)* RODENT FAMILY

Size: Overall length about 12 in (30 cm). The male is usually larger than the female.

Breeding: Three or four families may be reared during the breeding season which is from about April to October. There are usually five babies in a family and they are born blind and naked in a small nursery chamber lined with dry reeds and grasses. This chamber is dug just off one of the many burrows in the riverbank. This system of burrows will have an entrance both above and below the water level. Occasionally the female may choose to have her babies among the roots of a willow tree or even a disused bird's nest at ground level.

The babies open their eyes on the tenth day and are at least two weeks old before they eventually leave the burrow. At first, baby water voles are very reluctant to enter the water, which must surely look very wet and cold after the warm snug safety of their nursery nest. However, after some encouragement from mother,

they plunge in and quickly become little experts at swimming and diving. By their third week, they are quite capable of looking after themselves.

Habits: The water vole is often known, though incorrectly, as a water rat! Consequently, this inoffensive creature is given a bad reputation it does not deserve. Plump, thick-coated with a short nose and tail, it resembles a miniature beaver, quite unlike the sleek short-coated, long nosed and tailed common rat which is also found living along the riverbank.

Although the water vole is thought to be mainly nocturnal, feeding chiefly at dawn and dusk, it can often be seen feeding during the day. Its food consists of snails and insects with a preference for plants, grain, grasses, fruit and . . . a particular fondness for salad sandwiches.

The water vole is a rather shy creature but, like most animals, its behaviour is not always predictable. Even though the water vole is short-sighted, its very sensitive sense of smell will make it aware of any close presence. So, imagine my surprise when, while fishing from the riverbank one day, I turned around to discover a little water vole munching away at one of my salad sandwiches. Not having webbed feet, it was able to hold the sandwich in its forepaws like hands. It continued to nibble away within an arm's

length of me for some time before eventually waddling off to disappear into the undergrowth. Whenever I fished from this spot again, I would leave a sandwich, a salad sandwich, a little to one side and away from my own. I was seldom disappointed, my little riverbank companion nearly always turned up for lunch.

Although it doesn't hibernate, food is sometimes stored in one of the chambers in case it cannot get out to feed during bad weather.

Inoffensive though it may be, the male will fight ferociously in defence of its home territory. However, its threatening display of rearing up on its hind legs is usually enough to frighten off any intruder. Occasionally though, a more determined enemy may dare to do battle. It is then that the males in the family will engage the enemy, usually one at a time, until it withdraws, thoroughly disheartened and exhausted.

Dipper *(Cinclus cinclus)*

DIPPER FAMILY

Size: Length about 7 in (18 cm). The male and female are alike.
Breeding: The nest may be built in a crevice or hole in a bridge, a wall, a building, a tree, a bank, rocks, almost anywhere provided it is near the water. It has even been known to nest behind a waterfall. The small and somewhat dome-shaped nest is built by both parents and made of moss, grass and lined with dry dead leaves.

Three to six white eggs are laid, usually towards the end of March, and incubated by the female. Both

parents tend to the needs of the babies which will fly when about three weeks old. Two families are normally reared with sometimes a third.

Habits: The dipper is an unusual bird in that it swims but does not have webbed feet and, although it resembles a typical perching bird, rarely perches at all.

Fast flowing streams and rivers are this bird's favourite haunts. One, or perhaps a pair, will keep to a particular stretch of water and here seek the crustaceans, water insects, snails, tadpoles, small fish and fish eggs which form its main diet. For these, it will dive using its short powerful wings and legs to swim underwater. It will sometimes actually fly into and out of the water without a pause. It is believed to be able to remain underwater for as long as thirty seconds but a dive is usually of no more than a few seconds. Its flight is rapid and low over the water. When standing it constantly bobs its head and then its tail alternately, thereby possibly giving rise to the name 'dipper'. Or maybe it is so named because it is constantly taking 'a dip' in the water?

However it came by its name, it has become the adopted symbol of the county of Devon and I would believe by now, the adopted symbol of good fortune by a holiday-maker to that county some years ago. I was making a study of this bird at the time and waded into the river to avoid some overhanging branches and get a clearer view of a dipper through my binoculars. Returning to the bank, I spotted an unusual object almost hidden by the undergrowth at the water's edge. I couldn't make out what it was at first. Carefully picking it up and wiping away some of the mud, I found myself in possession of a very wet and very soggy wallet. After several hours gently drying it off in an oven, I was able to

examine the contents and discovered some money, bankers cards and all the usual things one keeps in a wallet including, fortunately, a driving licence which gave me the owner's name and address. The wallet and its contents were duly returned to a very surprised, relieved and delighted owner.

Bank Vole *(Clethrionomys glareolus)* RODENT FAMILY

Size: Length when fully grown about $5\frac{1}{2}$ in (14 cm) including about $1\frac{3}{4}$ in (5 cm) of tail.

Breeding: Baby bank voles can be born at any time of the year depending on the weather and availability of food. However, the middle months of the year appear to be favoured. Three to six babies may be born in each litter. They are born blind and naked. By the time they are four weeks old, their eyes are open and they are fully furred and ready to leave mother and start their own families.

The nest is made of grasses, moss, wool and feathers, woven into a ball, and may be found both above and below ground. Occasionally a disused bird's nest is used, often high in a tree.

Habits: The bank vole and its close cousin the field vole, are often mistaken for one another. They will often share the same countryside and their habits are very similar. The bank vole's tail, however, is usually longer and its coat much redder. It is sometimes known as 'red mouse'.

This little vole is generally thought of as a hedgerow dweller. Nevertheless, it is an expert swimmer and diver, and feels quite at home among the more recognised waterside dwellers.

Much of this vole's time is spent tunnelling just below the surface. The tunnels can sometimes be traced by the slightly raised surface of the ground. It creates a multi-tunnelled system of runways, which enable it to travel, safely, quite considerable distances without exposing itself to the many creatures that would otherwise prey upon it above ground. Unfortunately, where these runways are dug along a riverbank, rainwater seeping in can often cause parts of the riverbank to fall away.

Bank voles, of course, must frequently leave their cover to search for food. Their diet is widely varied. Seeds of all kinds, plants, bulbs, roots, fruits, grasses, grain, insects and even the occasional snail will be eaten with relish. The prospect of a meal will usually overcome the vole's natural caution. Once, within only a few minutes of my trimming back the wild rose by the field gate, a little bank vole appeared and headed with unerring aim, straight for the cutting with the hips, some three or four feet (1 m) from the hedge. Finding the hips too firmly attached to the twig to pull off then and there, it decided that this exposed position was no place to stay for lunch. So, carefully judging the centre for balance, it picked up the cutting and carried it with commendable effort back to the safety of the hedge.

Kingfisher *(Alcedo atthis)* KINGFISHER FAMILY

Size: Length about $6\frac{1}{2}$ in (16 cm). The male and female are alike.

Breeding: Normally six or seven white and rather roundish eggs will be laid sometime between April and June. These will be laid on bare earth in a small round chamber at the end of a slightly rising tunnel. This tunnel may be between one and three feet (30–90 cm) long, which the parents dig out themselves. They drill into the riverbank with their powerful bills and

then shovel the loose soil backwards with their feet. Both parents share the incubation period and the rearing of the chicks when they hatch.

By the time the chicks are three weeks old, they are fully feathered and leave the nest chamber to seek their fortunes in the outside world. As with most young hunters, their first and inexperienced attempts at fishing for themselves seldom meet with much success. The parents, therefore, will continue to help support them until their fishing improves. Two families may be reared each year.

Habits: The dazzling colour of the kingfisher is almost unbelievably beautiful, the iridescence of the plumage causing it to change colour with every movement. Its flight is quick and low over the water as it travels between its various perches from where it is able to survey the river scene. Should something of interest catch its eye in mid-flight, it will hover like a humming bird.

Any small water-dwelling animal life, from beetles to tadpoles, will be eaten, though its favourite food is fish. For these it will dive, with eyes closed, to grasp the fish in its bill. Then, it will fly out of the water and alight on a nearby perch. The dive is over so quickly that, but for the disturbed water, it is sometimes hard to believe that the dive had happened at all.

Although this little bird may take fish almost as large as itself, it is by no means a reckless fisherman. I observed a kingfisher, perched on an overhanging bough, watching a large brown trout sunning itself in shallow water. After a while, it flew off, only to return seconds later. Thoughtfully tilting its head, it seemed to be making a re-assessment of the situation. Eventually, deciding that perhaps, after all, discretion was the better part of a large meal, it flew off upstream.

Index

The riverbank is a most exciting and rewarding place for anyone interested in watching wildlife. Creatures from the surrounding countryside as well as the riverbank dwellers can be found there. They all need water and will therefore eventually come down to drink from their nearest river, stream, lake or pond.

Early morning and evening is usually the best time to watch but there is always something of interest happening during the day to make watching worthwhile. Find a secluded spot and remain as quiet and as still as possible. Above all, you need patience – the animals are there but will only emerge into view if they feel safe. The slightest noise will travel far across the water and warn them off.

Please remember, not all riverside pathways are open to the public. Most waterside land is privately owned and permission must therefore be sought before you enter.

To find out more, visit the local public library, which can usually recommend books and supply addresses of the local wildlife and conservation societies.

 Printed in England. ISBN 0 85503 072 0. B203